Grief Sweat

Grief
Sweat

Jody Aliesan

BROKEN MOON PRESS · SEATTLE

Single poems first appeared in *Crab Creek Review* ("omens" and "fate"),
in *IMAGE* ("unified field theory"), in *ERGO!* ("April Fools Day" and
"Beltane"), in *Literary Center Quarterly* ("entrance"), in *Prune Alley
Quarterly* ("Uath," "summer solstice," and "sitting next to ruins"), in
Poetry Northwest ("divination"), and in *The Written ARTS* ("aurora,"
the second "grace," and "winter solstice").

Printed in the United States of America.

ISBN 0-913089-19-2
Library of Congress Catalog Card Number: 90-86377

Broken Moon Press
Post Office Box 24585
Seattle, Washington 98124-0585 USA

to the neutral angels

Seeing into darkness is clarity.
Knowing how to yield is strength.
Use your own light
and return to the source of light.
This is called practicing eternity.

Lao Tzu

Contents

Acknowledgments

The writing of *Grief Sweat* was encouraged by a New Works
Award from the King County Arts Commission's 1988 Indi-
vidual Artists Program. Individual poems received publication
support from the King County Arts Commission, the Seattle
Arts Commission, and Bumbershoot (the Seattle Arts Festival)
Written Works 1990. My thanks to the editors, jurors, commis-
sion members, and staff.

Thanks also to the editors of the journals where other pieces first
appeared.

The poems "fate" and "seven gates through the underworld"
owe a great debt to Liz Greene's *The Astrology of Fate*.

I am grateful to the Native American tradition for the presence
of Coyote.

Dark Angel

Not knowing the way,
I move forward on the way,
with hands outstretched,
with hands outstretched.

Native American
(tribe unknown)

entrance

stand quietly now
breathe slowly
until you get used to the dark

you will see nothing
but it will press less closely

your arm nearest your heart
raise it to that side
step sideways to that hand
palm out fingers loose
you will find a wall

warm or cool
damp or dry
rough or smooth

lean into it
feel it down your arm
against your cheek your lips
the side of your foot

stand straight again touching it
easily

breathe

step your left foot ahead
asking the ground
now the other foot
slowly keep walking
fingers lightly on the wall

this is the way in
also the way out

♦

here is an opening
it has no floor
you have traveled down inside a branch
of the tree of life

now

step in
      fall
          feather
               down
                    long
                        shaft

into deep dry moss
sinking
springing

lie still
easily
until ahead you see
curved edge of light
first limb of the moon after earth's shadow
round door barely open

now

with your heart hand again
slip fingers into that bright crevice
pull darkness toward you

what do you see

equinox

dawn breaks long over the valley
harvest moon stands slow at sunset
even so strange charge called passion
stares at us until we wake to its gaze

just as it wanes

just as the steady glow begins to cool
instinct becomes self-conscious
before it feels awkward what was
assumed rebelling against expectation

glaring coldly as it turns its face

you had your chance to stay awake
while the heat was strong and now
there's no holding back no going back
we move into the dark

Thursday

it all began in the city where my closest womanfriend
said *I'm taking you out on the town* which for us
meant chocolate truffle cake at a pastry shop

driving up 10th to the Hill she told me
don't stop too close behind a big truck
you can't see around it

love is like that

                                     we parked across the street

from an ice cream store and saw on the sidewalk
a big telescope I thought was a dummy to advertise
some planetarium show because of the vinyl housing
but no these optics are real *it won't bite you* he said

go ahead and look

                                   and there was Saturn

big as a dime on a tablecloth rings and a moon the man
eager and serious in a black t-shirt was offering
views of Saturn and Jupiter for fifty cents
we came back later for Jove and

three more moons

                                   there on the pavement

7

the sky blacked out otherwise by shop street traffic lights
teenagers with smokes and radios sitting on the wall
right behind us summer crowd edging by single file
in their running shorts smell of coconut oil
on Broadway in the middle of town

I had to come in to see out

Why Coyote has a haunted look

Coyote came back from the wild and found his mate had taken another lover. He could not stay with her anymore. So he stayed in other lodges with too many people and too much noise. One day, driven by grief, he entered her lodge while she was out. It gave him comfort to sit on the bench they'd chosen together, gaze around him at the quiet things which spoke of her way, and smell her food and coffee. He climbed upstairs to kneel at the bed, press his face into her pillow to inhale the smell of her hair and slide his muzzle down the sheets to where her sex seeped its fragrance into the cloth. Never mind that there were other smells. It gave him some peace from the great sadness that filled him sometimes with such pressure he wanted to scream, wanted it to burst him, tear him open and bleed him away.

It wasn't long before he went there again, and again, always watching outside to make sure he wasn't seen, always listening inside so he could slip out the back if she came home. But mostly it was when he knew she would be gone and he could sit down, lean back against the wall, stretch out his legs, breathe deeply, and pretend for awhile it all hadn't happened. If he ate a little food from her baskets or smoked from her pipe, he thought it wasn't much and wouldn't be missed, and besides she would give it to him if she were there. It helped him survive his desperation and homelessness.

One day as he sat on the bench he saw a letter on the small table in front of him, open and facing up. Without thinking, he began to read it. It was a love letter to her. It came to him then, all the craziness stored up from trying to forget her evasions, her silences, the craziness of not knowing what was going on, not knowing what was real and true. So he read the letter. It was compensation. It was something solid he could trust. The paper, the handwriting. But that night in his borrowed bed he couldn't get the words out of his mind. He couldn't sleep for the sorrow and rage that someone else could speak to her so tenderly. He was obsessed with memories of old conversations, strange hints that puzzled him at the time but now rang with prophetic meaning. Dawn came and he wept for not sleeping.

But he couldn't stop himself from going back, and now he began looking for things that would tell him about this great injustice, as if by seeing and handling them he could work a kind of revenge, poison their happiness. Over time more signs were left of the unknown person. Underwear. A comb with different hair in it. A second toothbrush lying beside hers. Small objects unlike what she would bring home. Food she wouldn't have chosen. He couldn't understand how she could be with someone like that. He felt as the objects increased that he was being replaced. That her lodge was now a source of anger and pain and would give him fresh hurt whenever he came to it.

But he couldn't stop. Finally one day he found a stack of photographs on the table. They were taken in the bedroom, and he understood the use of the strange floodlamps and cords he saw in a box by the door an earlier time. Some of the photographs were black and white, of her lover lying in a provocative way surrounded by the folds of the sheets. Others were in color, of two bodies together. The last was of her face. Abandoned and ecstatic. Coyote left and never went back. He was given what he had been asking for. He hasn't been able since to get it out of his mind.

How Coyote learned what he needed most

Coyote's friends didn't know what to do with him. Some at first were pitying and sorrowful, but as days ran into weeks and weeks into months their forbearance wore thin and they began lecturing him, giving him blunt advice, even calling him names. To his face. Others, not friends after all, took undercover and sometimes open pleasure in seeing his pride finally broken, his belief in himself undermined. Once he walked into a meeting place and could tell from the eyes turned toward him that everyone knew. Then he heard one voice say *I used to think you were special, unusual. Now I know you're ordinary, just like me.*

Coyote listened to everything they said.

Some of them said *Maybe she's doing this to free you. Now you'll be able to find a* REAL *woman.* Others said *She needs to do this before she can promise herself to you. This will not last long.* One of her best friends told him *Hang in there as long as you can stand it. She doesn't know her own mind.* Still others said *Walk away. Let her find out what it's like to lose you.* One old friend counseled *Do what your heart says.* But he couldn't hear what his heart was saying. The din of all the other voices was too loud.

All he knew was that she kept calling to him, kept wanting to be with him.

At first this was not so. She was seeing her new lover nearly every night. He walked by her lodge each morning on his way to the fields and saw the second horse tied at the gate. She called to Coyote once a week or so with concern and apology in her voice, wondering how he was. One night she told him *I'm taking this new bond seriously because we're supposed to take bonds seriously, but I have doubts about whether it will hold.* Coyote responded like a tortured lover rather than as a friend. Ever afterwards he felt sure his reaching for her then probably drove her toward proving the new pairing would endure. It seemed as though everything he did went wrong.

But after awhile she began wanting to see Coyote when the new lover was away. Then even when he was around. Coyote couldn't tell whether she wanted to be with him for himself, because she missed what he could give her, what they had together, whether it was only because she felt guilty, or whether he was a piece in some game between the two of them, outside his understanding. He didn't know what was going on. But he answered to her, he went to her lodge, they talked, they made love, and although it was self-conscious now and haunted by the shadow of what they couldn't or she refused to talk about, the shadow of another presence falling between them, he drew from it what he could, he loved the best he knew how.

Which meant hiding from her much of what he was feeling.

One of the things he felt now was misunderstood. His friends seemed to want to see his plight as the simple one of Coyote's being abandoned, deserted, dumped, forsaken, that it was all over now and he was only fooling himself, feeling sorry for himself, wallowing in it, denying reality, that he should go on with his life, put this behind him, turn the page. One of them who had once been abandoned himself said *You haven't been singled out!* Or they said he should just get angry.

They seemed not to hear him when he tried to explain that it was not over, only more complicated. That he wasn't left, he was left hanging. That the shape of life was being drawn into a demand that she make a choice. And he felt a cold weight in the pit of his stomach: it was only a matter of time before she would choose the new and fresh over the old and flawed; he didn't have a chance or any hope in the long run unless he could behave flawlessly now. Every evening spent with her he felt he was on stage, compared, judged, as if she were looking for some reason to choose against him, some reason to choose one way or the other.

Coyote vowed that if ever he knew of anyone else living through troubles like his he would offer what he needed most right now: someone willing to hold him, without asking him what was wrong, without telling him what to do, without saying anything at all, while he cried.

How Coyote found some peace

Coyote couldn't sleep. Every thought led back to the source of his torment, and his memory, which had served him so well in the past, was now a questionable friend. When he did sleep, he woke to first an instant of infant freshness; then slamming down and through him came dread, a jolt of liquid lead in all his veins, a great toad sitting on his chest staring him down. It made him sick to his stomach. After awhile he slept every second or third night, when exhaustion muffled the thoughts scurrying around in his head and he was too tired to cry.

He lost his appetite. Food didn't interest him. More than that, it was as if something tightened around his throat when he looked at it. His body refused. He ate because he knew he had to, quickly, what he could put together with the least effort, the same things over and over again so he wouldn't have to think about it or make choices. Taste didn't matter, everything tasted the same or didn't taste much at all. He would have been relieved if he could have gone without it altogether.

His body began shrinking, evaporating away. It seemed so quickly his bones started to show, his ribs, and then his pelvis pushing its angles out from under his skin. When he lay on his back in the bath and looked down his length that great bone-mass rose higher than his thighs and belly, in fact he had no belly, only a great scoop out of his body, a hammock of hide hanging across from bone to bone. This frightened him. He ate more, but somehow never enough.

His feet scuffed when he walked now, his shoulders hunched. He avoided people's eyes, the strength in their glances cut and buffeted him. His hair hung flat and stiff. It broke in his comb, it came out in his hands, there was more gray in it. He pulled and twisted the same lock constantly until it was greasy in his paw. And his face was lined, his eyes puffy and blurred. He looked out of an expressionless mask. When he smiled at himself in the mirror, just to prove he could, it was an unholy grimace.

He began smoking tobacco, to ease the constant twisting angry heartpain. And to keep from crying, the helpless weeping that made him feel worse afterwards, weaker, his power leaking away. He knew where to find the smokes. People at intermission in theaters, or waiting at bus stops, or entering stores, often threw down nearly whole cigarettes. And when they didn't, there were many butts not all the way burned down, he could collect them in his paw, in his pocket, and then tear them open, gather the tobacco in a bag and roll whole cigarettes from it. They got him by, especially late at night and first thing in the morning, against the dread. And to start the day off with a feeling of some confidence, some sense that he was living his life instead of being lived by it, having it happen to him.

He was coughing now, coughing up gray lumps. Who knows what people's mouths left in that tobacco. But he didn't care. Even welcomed it. Coyote had learned there are fine gradations to desiring death: at the bottom, you want to die and you're getting ready for it. A little less desperation, you want to die and would make use of a chance if it came along. After that there's the feeling that with luck you might be developing a terminal disease. Or if you were, you wouldn't mind. On the next level you hope you'll be hit by a truck. Then it would be all right to be hit by a truck. The easiest is when you don't care whether you live or die. A balanced, peaceful feeling.

betrayal

Song of the Bald Eagle
we want what is real
we want what is real
don't deceive us
Crow

when seafloor slips out from under
slides beneath landshelf
no place to stand except among volcanoes

feeling rock snap underfoot
great shudder shivering its way up
soft shining plume-draped summit face

crumples   falls   crashes   rolls
lost in slow motion silence galactic time
slaps basin lake across ridge snouts
scouring off trees

enough

no this is just beginning now comes
straight toward you hot blast
dark breath out of deathmaw churning teeth

blown boulders rock bombs stones
gravel pebbles sandblast ash
grinding lungs etching eyes this rolls by

last powder lifting onto high wind stream
on its way around your life next year
it'll blow up behind you

what now

start walking no not out for help
back to where it came from first
through standing dead trees singed peeled

then all blown down gray valleys slopes
dust desert but for sweep of
shattered limbless lathe-rolled logs

ridge after ridge combed splinters
all pointing the same way until
still higher closer everything everywhere
blasted to bedrock nothing nothing

nothing

your heart plugs your throat
your stomach falls away

can you stand still can you keep yourself
from screaming staggering running
off a cliff thrashing writhing

all the way down hold your hands
over your eyes to keep them in your head
bite your arm better to bleed

than crack all your teeth at the roots
clenching back that howling
shriek   cry   sob   gasp

        of grief

no
you may think so at first
while your mind scrambles for high ground

while the hole in your heart tears more
delivering sacrifice forgiveness understanding
but you lie and you know it somewhere

down in that crater
you smile a false smile

that crack

begins it all over again

dark angel

to learn what I have to teach
you must be willing
to go without sleep and food
cry often helplessly with dread with
screaming in the back of your head

weak thin transparent shaky
torn your power seeping bleeding

you must be willing
to blame yourself for all of this
be obsessed with your failure
returning to the crossroads pacing
sifting the dust the same images
jamming your head until you want
to hit it against the wall

you will watch yourself over and over
do what shames humiliates demeans you
without being able to stop

frightened worried restless angry
punished harassed deserving it
unloved misunderstood pathetic
shunned excluded tolerated
frustrated defeated trapped resentful
do something fix it

whatever you do
will make it worse

broken empty sad remembering
something called pleasure joy in life
but it doesn't happen anymore
your hair will dull break gray fall out
your bones will show your face bloated
lined coarse ugly old

nothing to give your sight too blurred
from the sear of pain to focus
other people's lives shellshocked
rewired blown fuse can't concentrate
think clearly what's the name
of what I loved

stunned intensity can't decide
don't trust decisions every choice
seems wrong everyone closing in shouting

but nothing is real you watch
the dream from behind invisible wall
even your handwriting scrawls you've lost
your self your soul your faith a demon
possesses you now staring out your eyes
you've changed you'll never be the same

this will never end hopeless to try
to do something about it better to die
than live with this mind this
screaming darkness glaring light

are you ready

depression

'cause you survive
don't mean you grow

Jackson Browne

at one hundred fifty feet a diver breathing

ordinary airtank fights to hold
barest sense of simple thought what's subtle

isn't possible brain slows the inner ear
addles the world is spinning up is down

routine matters handling diving gear
either too difficult or unimportant anyway

decisions precarious any change in plan
not practiced in drill becomes emergency

effort of concentration drunk this way
exhausting afterwards the diver may be

limp for years

listen

All of life is a narrow bridge.
The main thing is not to fear.

Hebrew song

i.

nurse in a room of dying babies
looks out hour after hour at pale moon faces
of mothers fathers looking in

other side of glass
how arms ache

one shift carries in a braided rug
old floor lamp pillows blanket shawl
and a rocking chair

after that she leans back rocking holding
each night the one whose darkness hovers
nearest stroking humming kisses

on brow on ear or over heart
feels small arms loosen

till mothers fathers close their eyes
whispering whatever lullabies
through her mouth her lips whatever prayers

    till small ones know
    it's all right to go

ii.
madrona tree on edge of bluff
over beach over high tide water knows
it will fall already roots exposed but not
when or whether storm will tear
last hold or only daily trickle of sand

below it they step over boulders pools
he tells her how in concert the conductor
had a stroke kept beating time musicians
playing slower and slower someone
finally stood led him offstage

how sole survivor of an old quartet
sang at third one's funeral found a note
just as his heart failed held it fast
all the way down to floor beach water
ending faithful to his song

iii.
so we lie cradled
on bedshelves watching

through ceiling windows
moons passing

holding between hands
small soft comfort

leaning back on knees of earth

giving up
our arms falling

listening
letting the shudder come

Candlemas: late nor'easter

came quietly snow small light no wind
but no stopping I could tell
from the beginning it was serious
next morning windows over my bed
white canopy icicle fringes
every day longer crystal chamber
clear bars glass daggers to the ground

even ivy leaves blackened brittle
winter wrens leaving solitary
to flock for comfort early robins
hurtling stiffly onto branches
crying out bird tracks either side
of my eyes growing longer my hands
snakeskin my hair broken grass

veined with its own ice I could sleep
forever without dreams smiling
into last drifts but some voice urges me
make soup sit closer to the fire
wear a cap to bed this is the way
love goes and goes blood's heat
into black night all we have

each of us soul's candle long
as any sword   heart's pulse
steadier more faithful than any
lying promise of mild spring
parable: another day after this one
and maybe yet another after that
to learn what we have to learn to stay alive

for yourself only

great millstone of heaven
grinds exceeding slow exceeding fine
through eye mouth birthhole pass
whole worlds whole universes pearls
on a string breathe in breathe out
expand decline back to twine
again long heartbeat trail
of milky dust ash fading

not rungs on a ladder steps rooms
in a school no falling failing
only deep swim mouth wide open
into thick smoke blowing
from seafloor vents in lava light
every cell changed by that strange food

or a tree sensing newbuilt fence
wire tacked to its skin no walking away
sighs flesh through sharp web
fatemesh takes it to breast
until only rust leaves hatched
patterns in heartwood

so our visions grow tender
bubbles trembling breath then
skin collapses groaning once more
life blown into tightening membrane
of hope love search for an open bowl
new fed baby learning again
we're not made to fly turning back
to that breast whose teat

is a hole sucking hub of old
wheel mounted on skullstones
drawn by two gray horses striding boat
our song only wind through dried
tendons bare ribs of beached whale
our rhythm hearts breaking beating
two unlike hammers one anvil
one hammer two anvils
ringing into dark

grace

The hand is full of memory.
Very little is forever.

Kiowa

we turned away from beach into woods again
through that abandoned farm most times
up a lane along rosehedges south of the house
but this sunny late April afternoon

it seemed right to sidle through orchardgrass
accept some rhubarb from the only plant
left in the garden and walk back between
house and outbuildings same way as morning

passing by a shed something stopped my eye
closed door window pane sky sun glare
and behind it beating against hot glass
a hummingbird wings slow enough to see

we stopped I pushed door open stood aside
but the bird was too tired to notice any change
or remember gaps in siding how it got in
after that something happened all I can tell you

is I watched myself do it watched myself slowly
slide through doorway around behind
into dusty shadow where wings flapped and fell
against bright window ledge watched my hand

slowly close fingers around wild frailness
fingertips barely touching shoulders breast
feathers beat once more feet touched my palm
it turned toward me made one small sound

I watched my hand slowly move around
to the opening just as we cleared the door
the hummingbird burst away into apple trees
I stood holding fingers stunned around nothing

their tips just beginning to feel how soft
and light something was beginning to recall
something about a pulse along my thumb
my friends both shouting and me just coming to

out of Sumer

two words left to us
from the oldest writing:

Eden and *abyss*

sometimes abyss comes before Eden
dark shadow gorge cliffwalls too steep
too deep to see bottom even lying belly down
head hanging over verge vapors rise
from somewhere below breath of mirror face
looking up from other side tunnel end
crevice edge crack of doom

                              low thunder rolls
          up desert from the east
          moon's shadow rushes huge across the land
          strikes from behind us shrieking
          both horizons orange
          between them in an indigo sky

               black disk hanging
               white hair writhing
               scalp blood glittering

          around us silver ashes falling

shadow lifts sweeps suddenly away leaves us
gasping on the rim black faceless face
opens blinding white now
nothing will ever be the same

is this where we look for the garden

climbing down steep walls after first step
handholds appear scrawny shrub roots
after dead end chimneys opening on nothing
now hand foot pressure sideways down
inch by inch feet find rock find earth
after nights spent on ledges listening
to body water rolling into silence
now soft mist echo of a stream in trees

we are never happier than when we are happy again

Thank You Even for This

The harder you hold on,
the more the rope burns.

Viktor Frankl

thank you even for this

> The orphic insights of the disturbed
> are the hardest to tolerate.
>
>   Hortense Calisher

when he came stamping around my cabin
in the dark of that deep snow morning
shining his flashlight into my windows

up in the sleeping loft naked I said
are you going to sit here like a trapped
animal till he walks through the door
or will you go down and face the situation
my nearest neighbor a half mile away
through the woods and no telephone
on the island

      why do I attract this
      what have I done to provoke this
      what am I doing wrong
      what's wrong with me

      you attract what you fear

      if you want to know why you are here
      what you have come here to learn
      look for what repeats itself

courage lives in the stomach say the Nandi
of Kenya but there are times when it is
not at home and then the stomach is sour
something stalks toward us in the night
and we can only stand and bark

my shape shrinks inward a movement
clear only to me and my stomach burns

I have no stomach for this

       I have seen the evil eye
       and it is singular
       it smoulders out of a misshapen
       mask of malice the Salish say
       those who refuse to act for the good
       of others have a stomach of stone

       try not to hate it
       this is not a spiritual prescription
       but a practical one
       your hate gives it entry into your mind

so I pulled on clothes climbed down the ladder
stood as tall as I could in the flashlight beam
arms crossed over my chest and said
I've had enough
I want you to leave and never come back

he left
I was amazed

♦

run icy dirt road to the schoolhouse NO
white dog was with him and there it stands
turn back to the mountain HE CAME THIS WAY
where else to go his cap on a branch
in the alders an owl calls a clearing holds
neighbor's house counsel my story in the wings
of the main drama before day's end
four strong people with a twelve foot rope
guide him over the water to meet the sheriff

I WASN'T THE ONLY ONE IT WASN'T JUST ME

you were right to turn away do not
take on another person's soul
now cease this judgment of self
cease this condemnation of self
this is not a matter of blame
this is a matter of recognition

•

he came back
            I heard
                        was sent away again
that night after the thaw my mind rehearsed
the way it practices for stovepipe fire
what I would say if he showed up here
how to slide to the ground from my bedloft window
even how to kick him off the ladder
                        until my body hurt
            I went to bed
and dreamed

a stable system
expects the unexpected
is prepared to be disrupted
waits to be transformed
open to change
open to death

at the pit of my stomach
I am carrying a kitten
I leave where she is uneasy
no place to put her down

in a theater aisle
we witness a beating
her claws pierce my belly
I push outside to find
safe quiet place near trees
under shrubs by the foundation

something happens

I am robed in long cloth and a turban
from all around people of many colors come
draped in soft magenta purple blue they sign to us
we flow in their procession celebrating
past multitudes sitting gathered on a hillside
the kitten content to ride on my open palms

a man stands up to testify I RECOGNIZE HIM
he shouts

> *I thought courage was holding on*
> *now I understand*
> *it's letting go*

Grief Sweat

                                    Victory
          you know requires
Force to sustain victory: the burden is never lightened,
          but final defeat
Buys peace:

          Robinson Jeffers

traveler

for two nights after you stepped out of time
I set out food and water in my best bowls
left them on stones with sea shells cornmeal
to say goodbye ask guides to lead your feet

first night I laughed with you remember next
wept fiercely last I would see you in this life's
body your firelit skin your glittering eyes
waiting their flames for me to catch my

breath   waiting for me to laugh again at your
teasing sly sidelong glance through parted
starlight blanket as you slipped through
never mind I said *I'll catch you on the other side*

first morning bowls lay overturned I thought
by some night creature but second day
no one had touched them did you hook up
the cloudflap and leave with nothing to eat

well you still had a lot of fat on you
you'll be all right

Uath/six years

when deaf people speak the stronger
their feelings the smaller and slower their signs
not waving of arms but most subtle intense
turn of wrist
                our eyes spoke like that
the day we recognized each other
but all this month of maytree hawthorn whitehorn
virgin's tree month of ritual chastity
before midsummer rites we are parted
by land and water and time

                        on my way
to island log cabin post office close
beside gravel lane green tunnel road
grows a hawthorn tree I pick
sprigs of small white five petal flowers
supposed to hold my female fragrance
to wear in a buttonhole until they wilt
or send pressed in my mute letter to you
as it crosses yours to me in the postmaster's
hand

that night of hammering rain
and trembling thunder across the channel
with Tony in his Nova Scotia dory
telephone on the other shore your voice
almost too much to bear an hour home
of pitch and swell and the boat's surges
gray slanted rain a few distant lights I let
tears come my face already wet
hardly slept till dawn for my blood's high
whine

    last midnight walked through trees
to clearcut airstrip opening to watch
Saturn rise in Scorpio
                    planet of completed form
concreteness in the sign of passion
your soft tone in my bones now your heart
pulsing in the south with red Antares
as white petal drift of star clouds blow
in the earth's slow-turned gesture of longing

omens

The consenting sets one free.

Mary Renault

when
after you asked me to lie with you on the floor
where some breath moved from the window as day thickened
to night during that long hot dry spell
and I said no I was all right on the mattress
fitful from long desperation for relief of rain

you spoke in a quiet almost tearful voice
your loosening

before
the alarm in my blood rolled me down to your side
before the thunder from even that most gentle show of light
ran slamming into my chest something lifted me
grabbed me by the scruff of the neck upright
a few inches off the bed where a cool wind blew
through my head and whispered into my ear

just keep loving

now
my mind sifts through sweepings for reasons
probes my guts for a sign picks at locks at scabs
paces between records and strategies casting out lines
ringing the bell consulting the stars pleading with dreams
and crying into the night

but my heart rocks steady in an open lap
where a head can rest and hair be smoothed
where everything will be all right whatever all right
turns out to be

so
that morning when the raven flew exposed across
the clearing whistling wings with every beat
crying loudly we wondered whether to bless or warn
when the corn you husked carried an ear within an ear
and the great ships glided ghostlike in the strait
was simply the next of the rest of the days I will know you
hot or cool dry or fertile glare or shadow harsh or cradled
my fretful mind trusting into quiet my heart

finding open is full

Autumn Equinox, rain

fate

you who dismember decompose dissolve disintegrate
with your unseen hand its letters on the wall
this fruit I must eat is it of my own sowing
or left to me from someone else's field
am I helpless except to swallow it

groping for your clouded ambiguous intentions
launched in fogbound tide channels circling to find
invisible landing strip in the forest holding on
outside the plane on its running board
screaming into the wind

                        you are said

to have no design only boundaries unfoldings
both necessary and just sometimes I cannot help
myself sometimes I can often I think I shouldn't
sometimes I must your vessel whatever I do
let go lean off fall away or fly

your name

is liquid elusive as love compulsive as orgasm
we meet in old wild barren places heath
or treeless mountaintop mouths of caves
white robed mist clothed spinner of flesh earth bones
rocking loom of twofold thrusting
heaven wheel deep water web

you

are stronger than desire determination stronger
than reason duty principles or good intentions
stronger even than faith your wisdom in despair
surrender death your secret whatever holds me up
when I cannot stand whatever holds me fast
to my own promise

at last my pride is gone my will is yours

October

aurora

on stretches of sea ice around my heart
I stalk a white bear and her cubs

helpless in blown snow but infrared
of need senses heat in their footprints

mother shaman helping spirit teach me
to disconnect my bones fall out of skin

dive to seabottom show me a sign so strong
this grief will molt from me blow into foam

darkness whiteout I move between voices
of landward cliffbirds and seaedge surfbeat

watching wind angle in my parka fur
bending down to feel for snowridges

my compass wandering listlessly my radio
in panic sunrise sunset in one motion

stars wheeling free of the horizon every
landfall a mirage

                    what do you want
she howls ice booming in all directions

release from this hole the frost is chewing
beneath my ribcage I cry

look up she calls
your lover plays a torch against the sky

tender and tremulous whistle gently
for the lights to come near

and I heard you say
just as you did that night to lay

your love between me and the shadow
to rest in it

Hunter's Moon

seven gates through the underworld

i.

look back to name the death-flower picked
what small thing opened gates of earth
beneath you dark lord's chariot arriving
any redemption ecstasy may hold
is at the price of that rape rupturing

ii.

no altars to rulers of the underworld
each living thing holds its own
seed of death every act of love every hope
for renewal transformation what has died
will not live again in the same way endings
beginnings built on corpses of the past

iii.

brought naked bowed low stripped down
scraped raw emptied of landmarks
in the presence of life-freezing eyes breath
of black holes fermentation decay
split off turned in devouring your own power
hanging on a peg over fissures in the ground

iv.

all you hoard must be given away
what you want most the one thing
you cannot have or only
through sacrifice of some cherished part of you
two small mourners come to listen while you suffer
but with no advice nothing to be done

v.

except ride the wheel back to the same place
without release to meet again again
incurable disease untreatable wound
twisted outraged face never healed except
through fire where all beliefs must die
where what cannot be changed must be accepted

vi.

only then will deeper change begin
blessed forgetfulness merciful emergence
do not look back do not recall this road
or lose all courage for the future
bring back riches but forget the price

vii.

(all this remains a secret
not because no one will tell it
but because no one believes it
who has not survived the fire)

November

Fable

One early summer afternoon the sculptor and the poet sat on a bench near trees speaking images together when a pigeon fell into the grass near them asking with its eyes whether they might have some food. They apologized for having none. As the pigeon flew away they noticed it took to the air strangely. Something hung down from its body as it flew. The sculptor and the poet followed it to where it fell in the grass again. Coming up from behind the poet closed hands quickly around its wings and turned the pigeon so they could see underneath. Twisted around its feet was a long piece of wire tangled for enough time that in some places flesh had grown swollen around it and in others toes had been squeezed off. The wire was once covered with black insulation which the pigeon had pecked off everywhere it could reach. The pigeon didn't struggle in the poet's hands. She nestled it against her body and draped her jacket over its head.

The sculptor and the poet agreed it was not possible to set the pigeon down and walk away. Instead they walked with it to the university biology building. But it was after working hours. Every floor was empty. Everyone had gone home. No one was in the ornithology wing except a worker in a lab who said he knew nothing about taking care of birds. So they walked to the school of art. From the woodshop they telephoned veterinarians out of the yellow pages but no one answered except one assistant impatient to leave. She said *We don't do birds.* The poet and the sculptor looked at each other. While he searched among the shop tools for something small enough she stroked the quiet pigeon lightly wondering whether it might die of fear or shock or the heat under her jacket before they could free it. The sculptor walked down the hall to the metal shop. The poet stood in the coolness of the doorway holding the pigeon away from her body so it could feel the air. Still it didn't struggle.

All of a sudden down the other end of the hall in noisy conversation came the small old sculpture professor and two tall students, one a lanky farmer whose leg wore a metal brace, the other a big solid crewcut man in a sweatshirt. The professor called out to the poet *What are you doing here so late?* and she said *I have a problem.* Instantly the three surrounded her and she simply lifted the pigeon's feet into view. At that moment the sculptor returned to say the metal shop tool cabinets were locked. But the big man just happened to have with him a pocket knife bundle of surgical tools he used when he was a soldier. With his thick hands he touched delicately around the pigeon's feet looking for a place where he could snip the wire without cutting flesh or pulling off another toe. The pigeon's wings jerked once but it did not pull back its feet. Gently the big medic sawed at the wire. The bird trembled. The farmer with the limp said *I know exactly how it feels.* The small professor's voice shook. He said to the poet *Now don't cry.* The sculptor's eyes looked long. The poet felt the pigeon's heartbeat in her palm.

Finally the wire sprang open. Slowly the medic unwound it from around the few toes. The feet were free. And limp. The bird's neck was limp. But its heart was still beating. The five people carried the pigeon out of the building and laid it carefully on the grass. Its head fell forward on its breast. The sculptor crept up slowly closer with a saucer of water outstretched and set it down. Nearby a car engine started and the bird raised its head alert. Suddenly with an explosion of wingfeather sound it flew up away over the building out of sight. The people looked into each other's eyes and nodded and went their separate ways without out speaking.

A year later on another summer afternoon the sculptor and the poet sat on a different bench in a courtyard beside the natural history museum. As they spoke together they gazed into a cluster of pigeons pecking at crumbs left on the flagstones. One pigeon caught their attention. It moved differently. It was missing some toes and its feet were marked by raised ridges of flesh. The sculptor and the poet touched one another's hands. The pigeon walked among the other birds.

December

winter solstice

Thinking only makes the heart sore.

I Ching

when you startle awake in the dark morning
heart pounding breathing fast
sitting bolt upright staring into
dark whirlpool black hole
feeling its suction

get out of bed
knock at the door of your nearest friend
ask to lie down beside ask to be held

listen while whispered words
turn the hole into deep night sky
stars close together
winter moon rising over white fields
nearby wren rustling dry leaves
distant owl echoing
two people walking up the road laughing

let your soul laugh
let your heart sigh out
that long held breath so hollow in your stomach
so swollen in your throat

already light is returning pairs of wings
lift softly off your eyelids one by one
each feathered edge clearer between you
and the pearl veil of day

you have nothing to do but live

grace

winter night of perigean tide
highest in nineteen years
both dark of the moon

and its nearest swing to earth pulling
us in your old blue pickup
down to the sound

walking between high seaweed line
and wave edges slow tow ebbing
great water swell back out to sea

great starless sky dark as the tide
hovering down to meet horizon seam
lined with island lights

then strong wet wind hit from behind
so we turned face into the rain
back to the pickup under parklit trees

and you heard it
low yelping laugh of a sea lion
rolling in the booming night

so much water so much sky
so much darkness plenty
of everything

New Moon
January

February light

this far north
the sun wraps itself around horizon
instead of climbing overhead
by midsummer every room in the house
sunlit before nightfall
so much shadowplay

floating down
feathering through clouds fog rain
light drifts sideways
softening edges
taking shadows away

turning green
shedding its spectrum until
backlit by this directionless glow
refracted through all the microscopic
drops of water lying among leafhairs
a blade of grass tuft of moss

incandescent
breaks your heart with intense
fixed gazing ancient innocent
knowledge of every shadow in your
corners   blessing these
without noticing

patience

Nothing is hopeless:
we must hope for everything.

Euripides

up in borrowed room by candlelight
sky-eyed gypsy turns ends of her hair
far to the north hunters sit for days
by holes in ice alert for first
sign but deeply without waiting

depth where she sits not cold white
clay sink quiet spider trapped at bottom no
dark skin of water in spun copper bowl
on tiles between a dead and living tree
floats mother leaves seed spray

floats underneath whose hands whose
face not solitary priestess not
brave proud heroine on her way
to the pyre but swollen pomegranate
drying on quiltfolds its seeds secret

she prays *teach me to care and not*
to care teach me to be
still beside this pool this dark
foot of the wall until heart's homing
knows this is the right path speaks my name

Last quarter moon
April

what travels fast as speed of light

after she visited her mother
in the halfway house we drove
four hours to the ferry playing
twenty questions is it
animal vegetable thing she said
her daughter stumped them all once with
a shadow

June

summer solstice

Gaeð a wyrd swa hio scel.
Fate goes as it must.

Beowulf

our wills
only rain blown against the glass
of a closed window we can't see inside
but we rail against the sash the skirt
of warmth and shelter rather stand
in the storm of what we think
we know we want

      let go says sage
and cedar burning in this clamshell
spirits of the west who break
against sea stacks moon skulls
who sluice through straits dissolve and suck
their feet from under trees rolling
bones on your lathe who teach
release forgiveness first
of ourselves be with us

in this high room by candlelight
after midnight fire on the beach drumming
long sun down after ravens ants
pick our eyes clean to see
time herself moon shooting across the sky
star circles spinning until we dive
into river of daylight come
to our senses the shock
of being lost
                    to learn

we've never been found

when we're lost
we know who we are

we're the only ones there

sitting next to ruins
watching swallows build a nest

a lot of water hauled and more concrete
to cast these cellar walls
now what's left a set of steps
with all the world for door

neighbor who felled my trees
for garden clearing answered *how*
do I get so much done in so little time?
I never hurry

we never knew the ferry landing levers
were so easy to pull until a fragile nun
replaced the man no brawny haul
no muscular thrust just a turn of hand

the white-garbed devotee who climbed
up over co-op shelves to fix
grimy compressor came down still white
oil only on his fingertips   it takes

only what it takes
a certain calm repeated faith
mouthfuls of mud dry grass
until it's done

June

Return (The turning point)

> Someone who goes with half a loaf of bread
> to a small place that fits like a nest around
> him, someone who wants no more, who's not
> himself longed for by anyone else,
>
> He is a letter to everyone. You open it.
> It says, *Live.*
>
> Rumi

Shadow of a small plane on the water, on wooded islands below.
Labored takeoff. Maybe too much weight. Her backpack full of
books and clothes from three seasons gone. Box of food, box of
papers, box of his sculpture. Typewriter. Don't mind much if
we crash. Maybe we will. Closing her eyes: *Do what You want
with me.* Then the island drifting under them, sandstone cliff of
the point familiar, breaking her stare. Pilot quieted the engine,
glided down to long flat meadow. *Thanks,* she said, *my neighbors
appreciate that.* Everything unloaded into a row on dry grass in
front of the shake-shingled hut built for waiting out the weather,
last fall for an hour in fog wondering whether next droning
sound would come down, no telephones on the island. Sunny
hot cloudless day, coming back.

Nothing to wait for, moving already into tall trees, she hears the
plane engine turn over and whine into the sky. Walking now
up gravel road with cemetery gate into deeper woods, hemlock,
cedar, fir, toward shining metal roof. He chose the color, lichen
green, will blend with cedar siding once it silvers, reflects heat
in summer. Elderberry closing in on the path, need to prune.
Woodpile still standing. Beach gravel around steps up onto the
porch. Backpack off, set box down. Now turn around for quar-
ter mile to landing strip again, two more times. Don't think.

Afterwards dip water out of rainbarrel, pitcher into basin, wash hands and face. Barrel walls lined with algae, need cleaning. He thought baking soda might slow it down. Sit for awhile outside on bench he made. Push mesh over barrel mouth into water for the yellowjackets, thirsty. Dragonflies. A house finch. Walk around to the empty garden, fill birdbath.

Unpack food into pantry buckets. Open pantry window for cool northside air. Screens he made. Eat something easy, too hot to stoke the stove. Climb ladder to mattress. Among the ceiling pine knots the comet his eyes first found. On the wall birthday drawing he made, retreating and emerging patterns side by side. Years behind, years to come. River water flowing away to sea, glacier melt coming down. Rustling outside, dry alder leaves drifting down through branches. Not footfalls. *No one knows I'm here.* Silence. Darkness. Sleep. Lock of her hair between her fingers, pulled across her mouth.

August

April Fools Day/Good Friday/First Day of Passover

> He is strongest who is most alone.
>
> Henrik Ibsen, *An Enemy
> of the People*

> ... but the truth, the first truth,
> probably, is that we are all connected,
> watching one another.
>
> Henry Miller, *Timebends*

kneeling on a pillow at an open window wind
blowing my breath flimsy curtains out over empty alley
over rooftop puddles aid car howling in the dark means

    help is on the way

candle in a brass ship holder swinging
wax spilling somewhere into seashell on the table
but now I find it on this paper my hand

    bishop at heaven's gate kept waiting
    while angel leafed through books

    I gave many fine sermons
    surely you have them listed
    I was honored by the church
    surely

      oh here said the angel you
    were the one who fed the sparrows
    every Sunday morning
    come on in

what small acts
in all our error will save us

> *freedom* the critic writes *means*
> *me first*
> *values are personal preference*

so I stop and snap my fingers to the music move
seashell under pendulum of candle shimmer
of wax over mother of pearl what do I believe in

> scholar of Holocaust at conference on evil
> says *cynicism means*
> *not only do we know nothing*
> *we have faith in nothing*

no one can save me but me so I'd best begin
painting a naked woman out her mouth a dying tree
root ball in her belly one root hair threading
blood from between her legs around her thigh to the ground
where a plant flowers with pruning shears a scythe
scar over her heart blown out candle on her head
but her hair a cape billowing streaming

                                        pain

here ship candle swings again
nothing to be done acting only prolongs it nothing
to do but sit with it as with a friend

> calling suddenly
> to say she loves you

open the window again turn up the music
candle wax all over the table now

                              what do I believe

        pendulum in phase space spiral moving
        can't help itself
        toward strange attractor

        central point

        steady state of no motion at all
        doing nothing
        sometimes the only thing to do

                              as we keep watch

over one another dancing to our heartbeats watching
as from light years away long distance call
loving as best we can every moment layered wax pearl
of memory overlapping handprints mark of blood

        we have very little time left
        said the Buddha
        therefore we must proceed slowly

to find closure both beautiful and true

        the chemist wrote
        I have had my conclusions for a long time
        but I do not yet know how to reach them

so this is the weaving swinging of human love
blown gauze curtain web on a rainy night street sirens
touching the bottom and farthest reaches of heart
not one of us can be copied or replaced
each new and wordless roothair tender tree
wounded in every breath bearing for awhile
without defense the brutal assault of us all

Beltane

if only one could
make or find a bit of
wisdom that turned
through a situation
or two would hold
still or still hold

A. R. Ammons

once again in a pattering of rain
the bonfires burn
and he comes to her his mother
they lie in a fallow field a garden ready for turning
or he comes upstairs to her
bearing his candle
and she opens her flower to that fragrant fountain
memory of all words ever spoken
in bed alone I offer tribute with my two hands

the sculptor offers windows into the earth
into the sky rests after labor
remembering how a child slipped her fingers
into his handprint another stroked
cement cast baby and next morning
someone left a branch of flowering cherry
now he sees sun flame under storm at setting
feels full moon rise hears robins in their song

in the beginning astronomers say all was the same:
uniform molten symmetrical and barren
the great fire had to cool
perfect symmetries break
before life could be
out of that brokenness
out of that imperfection we come
living best at a scale where everyone's hand leaves a print

so the universe seems
it may have no meaning
but this is marvelous: breathe and see
if we need meaning we must make it for ourselves
it's best to remember we made it
lest we take it too seriously
walk without desire or fear
carry your vision of vastness
a live coal in the palm of your hand

divination

For nothing can happen to birds
that has not happened before:
We, though, are beasts with
a sense of real occasion,
of beginnings and endings.

W. H. Auden

why does this black-winged beast surprise me
ancient people always loved a monster gorgons on the roofs
griffins guarding temples courtyard-dancing satyrs
all creatures of day but this painted demon stares
from wall of an empty tomb not one waiting
unopened till we break the seal to scent of cedar no
already looted murals peeling from wet heat of breath

mystery folk of perfume and color banquets of touch
changed after invasion *there is a moment when you are strong
and take what you want then comes a time when life
is forced on you* believed they came from a mysterious boy
with wisdom of seers born from a deeply plowed field
to teach them omens in entrails flight of birds

and here is bronze figure of a boy stretched long
as last light of day yes it says they named him
shadow of the evening protector of lovers
watcher of those who must travel alone at night
so when you ask me how I am I speak instead of leafshadows

trembling on sidewalks nested swallows echoing
in a parking garage cottonwood seed-snow in curbdrifts
and I would tell you of these crows their dusky passage

across this crescent moon if I could call you   too much
light this time of year so long to wait for comfort

May

falling out

Mankind has its lesser beauty
impure and painful;
we must harden our hearts to bear it.

Robinson Jeffers

so I will swallow this stone down empty pool
slow dream fall sand stirred settling gently
onto heartpalm cold steady weight
setting heels pressing soul into pavement pebbles
slide off my eyes keen hawk glare
slices mystery open pregnant membrane veil
bursts stagnant water cell painful love

I can step out

ballast under my ribcage river round
fire-darkened granite a chip on one side
from some blow shaping first face or tool
hardened clue-ball of twine a way out of mazes
this one unravelable

now so am I

it was under my head when I woke to ladder
of feathers found by eyes on the ground
throw them away out of third floor window
fluttering stairs set pillow stone
on a pillar pour oil on it boundary marker
holy circle of boulders embracing old bones
tophet of animals children at last

sacrifice completed

New Moon
August

unified field theory

It is not more light that is needed
in the world, it is more warmth.
We will not die of darkness but of cold.

from the journal of
Jenny Read, sculptor
1947–1976

October dawn between dark islands
only waves small wake of our wooden boat
bright dew on our hands we watched earth roll
into sun's fire sigh great star detaching
from far ridge trees one branch at a time

not bad

for ninety-three million miles away I see
why we worshipped praise light he said
lightning I said *moves from earth to sky*
three fingers thick heats airsleeve to five times
sun's skin passion bolt or another kind
of love at a distance lifts horizon's hem
night's comforter

exploding stars

blow coats of dust so thick but particles
pass through us without shrugging rings
around black holes both gravity and entropy

increase whatever they are cradle balls
on a blanket stretched between hands pull
we roll together in new ways but haven't found
enough whatever to bring us all back in

                                    everything's distributed

we're touched without feeling each leaf fall
so many leaves *somewhere on that taut sheet*
someone is pulling my hair she said *each time*
I walk past the submarine base I tap the gates
maybe someday they'll crumble
                                    just then

came to mind the bombs on a school playground
in Southeast Asia medics stopped
blood from one small girl but too much lost
their type not matched so with gestures eyes
they asked her playmates for help
                                    a little boy

raised his hand it wavered rose again
they laid him down pierced veins but he
shook sobs tears streaming his fist in his mouth
what's wrong interpreter asked turned out
he thought he was dying to save her life
why would he do that the medics wondered

                              because she's my friend

if we could select for that he said
                              it's a force

in the universe too it must be distributed
not just this animal this planet alone
what the lightning knows when seas begin
to quicken beneath it anti-entropic acts
not measurable yet not amenable to our tools
but maybe what's missing to bring us together again

                              after that

we rocked awhile light and darkness danced
patterns in small chop around the boat
we docked next island looking back spread wide
long opening arms of our wake kept folding
morning's silken quilt
                              far as we could see

Design by John D. Berry. Typeset by G & S Typesetters, Inc., Austin, Texas. Text set in Granjon, with Diotima and Diotima Italic for display. Printed on acid-free paper and Smyth sewn by Malloy Lithographing, Inc., Ann Arbor, Michigan.